I0487987

The Environment is the Meeting

Other books by Coleman Lee Finkel

How to Plan Meetings Like A Professional

The Professional Guide to Successful Meetings

The Total Immersion Learning Environment: Its Critical Impact on Meeting Success

War Stories from The Meeting Front

New Conference Models for the Information Age

The Environment is the Meeting

◆

Achieving Optimum Results For Your Program

Coleman Lee Finkel

iUniverse, Inc.

New York Lincoln Shanghai

The Environment is the Meeting
Achieving Optimum Results For Your Program

Copyright © 2006 by Coleman Lee Finkel

All rights reserved. No part of this book may be used or reproduced by any means, graphic, electronic, or mechanical, including photocopying, recording, taping or by any information storage retrieval system without the written permission of the publisher except in the case of brief quotations embodied in critical articles and reviews.

iUniverse books may be ordered through booksellers or by contacting:

iUniverse
2021 Pine Lake Road, Suite 100
Lincoln, NE 68512
www.iuniverse.com
1-800-Authors (1-800-288-4677)

ISBN-13: 978-0-595-40335-6 (pbk)
ISBN-13: 978-0-595-84711-2 (ebk)
ISBN-10: 0-595-40335-2 (pbk)
ISBN-10: 0-595-84711-0 (ebk)

Printed in the United States of America

To my dear son, Andrew Duke
in appreciation of his
love, concern and support

Contents

Acknowledgements

There are so many individuals with whom I have networked and from whom, over the years, I have learned. During my ten years with the American Management Association, they include such former CEO's as Al Nickerson of Mobil, Fred Borch of GE, Eric Johnson of Texas Instruments and Pete Scotese of Springs Industries.

I am so appreciative of my associates at The Coleman Center whose dedication, hard work and competence have made our facility such a distinctive oasis for meetings of every type. They make it a pleasure to come to my office every day. My thanks to Rob (Trey) Birdsong, our director; Sharon Herard, our sales manager; Chris Ripper, manager of facilities; Sharon Wright, our program coordinator; Eileen Finkel, our controller; David Sandberg, financial consultant, Sara Whitten, our administrative assistant who was so helpful in preparing this manuscript; Leon Stennett, evening facility supervisor and Nicada Blake, administrative assistant.

I have drawn continuously on the wisdom of Al Zeisler, President of the Integrated Technology Education Group. My appreciation, also, to our many clients who continue to favor The Coleman Center with their programs.

Foreword

This book is focused on small group meetings of under 100 participants typically 10-50 attendees. Its objective is to provide guidelines and concepts for assessing and judging the true value of the place in which you hold your sessions whether an internal or outside facility. These standards go far beyond merely providing rooms. They offer thoughts on meeting centers and their details in design, service, procedures that, in their inclusion, have been shown to add another dimension and greater productivity to a program with improved results not only for participants but meeting leaders.

Meetings are a way of life in our society. Government agencies, companies, associations, non-profit organizations hold them. A meeting is simply a process through which information is exchanged. Two people can have a meeting, or tens, or they can involve hundreds or thousands of people. For businesses, a meeting can be a powerful medium to broaden the thinking of employees, improve their skills and modify their attitudes. Ultimately, the results are to improve the decision process, to reach greater operational productivity and enhance personnel competence.

This book will concentrate on the small group meeting. Of the hundreds of programs held at The Coleman Center, the preponderance of these sessions is attended by fewer than 100 people. In discussions with leaders and administrators of these programs, they, too, point out that the majority of their sessions are for smaller groups. There are certainly meetings of great numbers of attendees but these programs held on the same subject occur infrequently. However the same training program for 25 people or less may take place 10-12 times in a year, each time to a different audience.

Regardless of the purpose of the meeting, there are common elements essential for their effective execution.

1. The skill with which the interests, needs, and problems of the audience are thoughtfully researched and the creativity with which the meeting design is developed to communicate that information.

2. The knowledge and competence of the leadership in communicating information and guiding discussion.

3. The efficiency with which the administrative responsibilities are executed (facility arrangements, participant transportation, badges, registration, workbooks, signs, handouts, place cards).

4. The environment of and services in the selected facility within which the meeting will be held.

This book will examine aspects of meetings that are, generally, not given sufficient attention (or even consideration) though incorporating these factors will contribute to achieving the maximum return on an organization's large investment in its meetings. Through reading these chapters, it is my hope that one will gain fresh insights and a broader perspective in the following areas:

1. An appreciation of the critical factors in a meeting that add to participant concentration, facilitate attendee interaction, reduce individual fatigue, permit greater attendee participation and enhance participant enjoyment.

2. How the learning environment in a meeting facility contributes to the success of a program while its services ease and make more effective the role of the program leadership and the

administrators adding a significant extra dimension to the outcome of sessions.

3. The inclusion of measurement tools to aid in evaluating elements of a program that, in their execution, will add to a program's effectiveness.

Coleman L. Finkel

1

Meetings As A Way of Life In Organizations

Meetings have been an integral part of human endeavor and progress since the beginning of civilization. Throughout history, individuals, face to face, have been communicating, solving mutual problems, making decisions. Scott Beaty, head of Shell Learning practice observed, "When you are face to face, you absorb a million data points". Basically, the word "meeting" implies any gathering of people where an exchange of information transpires whether it involves two people, tens, hundreds or thousands.

In early times, one primitive family group met another and shared information about food and shelter. When families joined together for easier living and greater security, they formed a tribe. Tribes became nations and throughout this evolving process the need to meet and communicate remained an imperative. People want to communicate in groups bounded by social, cultural and or business relationships.

Kings, emperors, popes, prime ministers, dictators, presidents, since biblical times, have employed meetings to advance their goals. In the book of Genesis, God asks Moses to call his elders together in a meeting and explain how their people are to get to the Promised Land. To this day, town meetings in New England are a quintessential form of self-government.

American colleges have relied on the lecture format as its form of a meeting. Professional associations hold meetings to keep members up-to-date on their operation as well as developments in their field of specialization. Older professions, such as law and accounting, are required by their laws to participate in a defined number of hours of instruction each year. In those educational meetings, these professionals upgrade their knowledge, thereby, increasing value not only to their firms but to their clients.

Another interesting example can be found in Kuwait. Here, the country's leading merchants organize a "diuanmiya". It is a meeting through which they exchange gossip and air gripes.

There are various goals that a meeting can achieve: communicate information, solve problems, develop skills, reach decisions, improve attitudes and motivate people. Any number of names may be used to identify a program: Board meeting, training session, staff meeting, product presentation, employee orientation, conference, seminar, convention.

U.S. businesses are becoming their own educational providers. They view their investment in human resources as important as their investment in capital and physical plant. Therefore, it is American business that is responsible for the concentration and upsurge of meetings. Organizations have found that, with the plethora of information available, face to face contact is one of the most effective approaches to update information and knowledge and to develop and expand skills. Only personal contact, uniquely through a meeting, allows the attaining of greater insights and meaning by virtue of non-verbal signs: eye contact, body language, gestures, facial expressions, tone of voice.

The U.S. Under Secretary for Travel and Tourism observed "Meeting are more important than ever in bringing the world together. Technology advances are distancing people from one another. Technology is no substitute for the human aspect". Or, as Boeing noted, "You can't send a handshake by Fax".

Ralph Paul Wurman in his book Information Anxiety writes "Everyday, we are bombarded with more data than we can absorb and understand. One way to siphon the information pertinent to one's needs and, further, to understand its meaning is through the process known as a group meeting. Here an individual can question, expound, exchange, explore information among a group of similarly concerned and involved individuals". Other forms of learning certainly have relevance such as reading, on-the-job experience, distant learning, attending talks, viewing videos. But, the meeting format is a primary, fundamental and special means of communication.

The need to continually learn is crucial to being able to cope with the ever-changing conditions that the business world is facing, including globalization. Because knowledge loses value over time, it is incumbent on organizations to inculcate a continuous process of updated learning. Peter Drucker, the late well-known management authority, points out "Companies will improve their quality through being known as a learning organization". As an extension of that thought, Tom Peters, writer on management, observes "The company that learns together earns together".

The give and take among participants in a meeting underscores the kind of intellectual stimulation and knowledge absorption by individuals that make meetings such a valuable and indispensable adjunct to our educational efforts.

Every meeting should involve learning as its goal. Participants, when they leave, must know more than before they came and become aware of how to apply that knowledge. If those goals are not achieved, the meeting is a waste of the participant's time. That waste is not a factor of the meeting process itself, but, of its poor execution.

Since individuals vary in their learning style and comprehension, the adept leader, sensing those differences, will adjust the discussion to allow for those variations. In his masterful book, A Mind At A Time, Dr. Mel Levine underlines the importance of allowing, in a learning program, for the various ways in which individuals absorb information.

As never before, organizations require and value the acquisition of new information and skills. The meeting stands as one medium-a unique, pervasive and superior group process-to impart that information and develop those skills. The fundamental source of "wealth" in the world is the knowledge stored in the brains of its residents. The same aphorism is true for the personnel of organizations. Meetings facilitate that "wealth" accumulation.

A goal should not be to eliminate meetings. Rather, we need to concentrate on how to optimize their conception, objectives, planning and execution. In doing so, we will truly augment this powerful medium for increasing the competence, knowledge and productivity of personnel at every level.

2

The Relationship of Program Success To The Facility In Which A Meeting Is Held

In many ancient societies, human considerations and architects' objectives met. Artists and scientists of the Renaissance shared a common belief: an individual is the measure of all things. They believed that a structure and its interior spaces were an expression of a person's vision of the fundamental <u>human</u> purpose of that structure. For example, the pyramids of Egypt were built to glorify the Pharaohs.

Consider the environment for that famous monument the Taj Mahal in Agra, India. It was built in the 17th century by Shah Jehan. In its totality of detail and aesthetics, he wanted a structure to represent his expression of love for a woman. The pavilions and marble mosque created a monument nestled among lotus pools and exquisite gardens. Here is a facility designed and built with a mission that visitors experience today with awe, though it is centuries old.

The first structure constructed with the needs of a professional group in mind was the Inns of Court. They were used by London's legal experts during the mid-14th century. Built of stone for quietness, these building stand today and are still used.

And so today, emotional, intellectual, psychic elements embodied in a meeting facility, must also be planned with a mission and strategy.

Consider how its design can help to transform the attitude and mood of the participant away from the distractions, the pressures, anxieties and problems of the outside world. The environment which, in every aspect, should say "You are here to learn, to think, to interact with others in a relaxed, pressure-free setting, designed to maximize your learning and growth throughout every hour of the day".

The late, noted Harvard behavioral scientist B.F. Skinner, in his book Beyond Freedom and Dignity, wrote the following "We are all simply a product of the stimulus we get from the external world. Specify the environment completely enough and you can exactly predict an individual's actions" Professionals who plan and lead meetings are growing more sensitive to the implications of Dr. Skinner's concept.

There is clearly a relationship between where a meeting is held and its impact on the participants and ultimately to the meeting's success. The Roman poet Manlius wrote: "Finis origine pendet—the end depends on the beginning". The end result of a meeting begins with the original decision of where your program is to be held.

A facility can make a substantial contribution to the final result of a program. The physical spaces can assist the attendee to learn or they can be a detriment to that process. The attendees become richer in knowledge, more motivated to want to apply the new knowledge back on the job. This process is enhanced if there also a pleasurable learning experience. That enjoyment factor can be attributed to the contribution of the facility design.

Certainly the meeting environment alone will not make a poor program a success. The meeting content and its leadership are the crucial factors in a meeting's outcome. But a learning-engineered center that relates the learning goals of a meeting to the supportive environment spaces within will increase the likelihood that participants, as well as the leadership, will leave with a sense of a mission accomplished.

There is a swelling chorus of dissatisfaction with meeting facilities. Letitia Baldridge, a former White House aide, now head of her own public relations firm, wrote an article titled "Why Meetings Can Be So Deadly". Ms. Baldridge made these observations "Taking stock of the environments in which these meetings are held and the sustenance offered up for enduring them proves one thing: American business people are sure tough. Whether it's the in-house conference room, the glossy chrome and steel boardroom or the rented borax ballroom of the hotel, the atmosphere of the average meeting is itself a severe test of the physical and mental stamina of its participants".

Kenniston Lord, a management consultant, wrote a book called "The Design of the Industrial Classroom". In that book, Mr. Lord points out that he has often wondered what it would be like to have a facility designed to accommodate the participants rather than have the participants and instructors adjust to the physical facility. He further indicates there are those who view a classroom as merely another room or converted office space. Lord expresses frustration at trying to help an attendee absorb information in an inadequate facility which all too often negates the learning process. Alvin Toffler, the well-known futurist, in his book "Future Shock" observed that our educational structures are racing toward obsolescence. He adds that very little thinking is being done about how to save or replace them.

There is a Japanese concept being applied today in the design of spaces. It is called Feng Shui. The approach relates the vision of the user to how spaces "speak" of its purpose. Planning is then accomplished so that every aspect of the place's environment meets the identified mission.

Perhaps not as esoteric as Feng Shui philosophy, there are many elements in a meeting facility that need to be researched and planned so that with its carefully crafted elements, participants are stimulated to learn throughout the meeting day.

One executive, interviewed for this book had previously attended a program in a meeting room of his company. The program extended for several mornings over a period of three weeks. He said "Every time I walked into that room I felt I was in purgatory. I couldn't wait to get out". His attitude obviously had an affect on his learning.

The American Society For Training and Development published a brochure titled "Succeed In Facility Planning". In that publication, these observations were made: "The physical environment can have a major impact on the success of any training program. No matter how well designed the program, regardless of how talented and entertaining your presenters, a good session in a poor environment might add up to a waste of time and money". Further a poor environment can cause eye discomfort, physical fatigue, difficulty in remaining focused, headaches.

The term "conference center" is being used indiscriminately today to describe any facility that has provided rooms for meetings. Unfortunately, many of these facilities are merely using the phrase as "buzz" words. They have not made the substantial changes in what is being offered hoping, though, those words will attract business. These places do not incorporate standards set by the International Association of Conference Centers.

As models of educational excellence, it would be easy to assume that our colleges and universities would be in the forefront of thinking and research on learning facilities. They might want to look at what ways can their planning and design of their environments contribute to increased student learning. Not so for many institutions!

The council of Educational Facility Planners published a study called "What Went Wrong". In this brochure they wrote "It is a tragedy that even now educational facilities are being planned on the basis of antiquated theories, false conceptions or conclusions derived from ignorance. Complacency and contentment with the status quo are incompatible with good plant building".

Jamie K. Reaser is President of Ecos Systems and a Certified Master Practitioner of Neurolinguistic Programming. In an article titled "How the Environment Shapes Learning" she wrote, "Trainers must be more consciously aware of the need to be more concerned and focused on where they are placing their meetings. Nurturing the environment in which their programs are held can make a significant difference in the success of a program. It is the environment that will shape the learning process for indeed that facility can either interfere with or enhance participant knowledge".

Even the American Institute of Architects, along with neuroscientists, are undertaking a research project, studying the affect of design on the human mind. They will look at how the design of a building directly influences the emotions, health and the minds of individuals. If we are to take further steps on optimizing the enormous investment in the dollars spent on meetings, it will be fruitful to pay further attention to how the total immersion in a learning engineered environment adds to the achievement of that goal.

The properly designed meeting environment, indeed, has "value", That "wealth" must be judiciously spent. For, if the intrinsic worth of a facility is not producing a significant contribution to a productive learning experience, then money is being misspent. The facility will influence the spirit with which an individual approaches a meeting. It is the totality of the environment that conditions the life of the educational activities that enfold within.

There are objectives that a judiciously planned meeting place must incorporate in its equipment, decor, room design, furnishings and technology. Think of how to include such factors in order to:

1. Encourage participant interaction and cross-fertilization of ideas among them

2. Increase and sustain a high level of concentration among the attendees

3. Reduce participant mental and physical fatigue

4. Provide a quiet, secure, private room for each program

5. Create an environment and develop services that promote an enjoyable, pleasurable experience for attendees

6. Support every need of the meeting leadership so that every facility-related problem is eliminated.

7. Prevent distractions

A meeting facility is the silent but essential partner in achieving not only cost effectiveness but also the maximum productive outcome of any meeting.

3

A Meeting As Community

Fostering the bonding of a meeting's attendees into a homogenous community of shared interests and objectives should be a primary goal for every meeting. To the degree that individuals feel "comfortable" and secure with each other, their participation in the structured part of the program will be facilitated as well as their exchanges during the critical informal times of the sessions. High performance meetings do not just happen. They result from teamwork created by a close communal feeling of a group working toward a common learning goal.

The formation of any group into a meeting creates a new society for its duration. It has characteristics of a democratic legislative body. There is a leader. The way of life is "codified" by rules of procedure and sets of values emanating from attendee conduct. The participants are deliberating in a self-contained room, drawing from their own resources to insure what they are doing is meaningful.

Michael Suk-Chwe is in the political science department of the University of California at Los Angeles. From his observations, he has concluded that communal activities, such as in a meeting, increase emotional and symbolic content, which, in turn, serve a positive, rational purpose. Mr. Suk-Chwe points out that those activities occuring in this "community" will further the cooperation among participants to their mutual learning benefit, increasing the bonding in their new "community".

A meeting group should imagine itself in a small new world or society. They are sharing an important common experience. That experience will result in maximum learning evolving from the security of being among others with shared interests. The comfortable exposure of meeting participants in their "community" facilitates the exchange and clarification of ideas and the reinforcement of knowledge gained. People learn most when they can connect with others in their group questioning, contributing, exchanging and solidifying the meaning and use of information. To the degree that "hostility" exists in a group, conflicts will reduce both cohesiveness and also their mutually supportive discussion.

In other contexts, it is apparent there, too, that camaraderie, a bonding into a "community" of shared goals have important results. The following cases have relevance for meetings as examples of how that communal feeling contributes to achieving shared goals.

Golf could be the ultimate example of the formation of a community for a period of time and for a stated mutual purpose. Four people form a relationship of camaraderie and trust that each will keep score accurately. They share a closeness and interdependence in a "new society" whether starting as strangers or friends. When the community disbands the group has bonded, living through a mutually beneficial experience.

In Hollywood, there is new facility called the Knit Cafe. Men and women may spend many hours a day here because of the quiet environment and the opportunity to meet with others with shared goals. They say that their joy results from the warmth and feeling of an old-fashioned small town community.

In the world of pastoral care, there is a term called the "ministry of presence". The help given to an individual in need comes through providing a "presence" and company by a sympathetic soul. The person needing assistance not only has someone with whom problems can be shared but also feels that there is an individual who cares about her/him. In a meeting, an objective should be to develop a similar "presence". Only here, there may be several individuals who provide that support.

In Buddhism, there are three jewels to be achieved: 1. Teacher 2. Teaching 3. Sangha or Community. In this community, there is love, interdependence, sharing. These qualities can be related to their advantages in the community engendered in a meeting. Here, the cohesiveness of a group, with a sense of interdependence, will help to spark discussion, benefiting everyone.

For conferences of hundreds or thousands of attendees, it is not likely that a feeling of cohesiveness can be achieved. In meetings of these sizes, a sense of space and alienation can occur as an individual sits as one in a sea of unfamiliar faces.

In remote activities such as in telecommuting or e-learning, though each certainly has advantages, many feel their downside is they breed a lack of "face time"—an essential part of a meeting. It is unlikely that the distance factor will produce the same kind of intimacy possible through the on site personal interchange of others in a group discussion.

A meeting facility can be a primary factor in engendering the cohesiveness of a group in a program. Once a person enters a meeting center, an orientation process enfolds for the individual that is emotional, intellectual and psychological as one becomes acquainted to a new, pressure-free, calming environment. Once this transition, shared by others in her/his group has been made, then this orientation should be sustained throughout all activities of the day. In this "cocoon", increasing familiarity with one's surroundings and its spaces engenders a comfort level with others. That comfort level, if sustained, carries over, during the sessions themselves, into attendee closeness and a feeling of the spirit of a community.

In a small group session, a different culture is established among attendees. It exists to accomplish and contribute to goals that no one could achieve alone. Through this commonality of purpose, it becomes easier for individuals to know one another, to feel free to participate in the session themselves as well as to share thoughts and questions with other attendees.

As a means to build the community, every opportunity should be taken to develop processes that make it easier and more comfortable for participants to learn the names and affiliations of the other attendees.

To facilitate the community esprit, here are several approaches to be incorporated. Some are obvious and are already in use, but the review can reinforce your approaches.

1. If it is a meeting in which not every one knows one another, use name badges with the attendee's first name in bold letters and the individual's affiliation noted.

2. Use place cards with the person's first name in bold letters. As discussion proceeds, individuals can then quickly identify the person asking a question or making a contribution.

3. At the opening of a session, though it takes time, have each person clearly introduce herself/himself by providing their name, title, company if necessary and a brief description of responsibilities. Even in a meeting where everyone knows each other, they are now forming another community. Suggest each person open with a comment such as some activity from their work that may be of interest to the group.

4. In the beginning of a meeting, when a person makes a comment, it is helpful if the leader asks the individual again to state name and affiliation.

5. Try to select a room that is square rather than long and narrow. The more square the room, the easier for participants to see, hear and identify with others in the group.

6. At breaks, arrange a separate area where your group can be together, thereby more easily interacting with others in the same group. Arrange an assortment of refreshments and beverages which will encourage participants to engage in informal discussions while relaxing with food.

7. At lunch, arrange seating in groups of 4, 5, or 8. Such table seating, results in individuals taking part in group discussions about the program, enhancing their familiarity with others. A table of ten is too large to foster a group discussion. It is more likely that people will talk only to the person next to them.

8. If team projects are used, rotate the teams so that attendees are exposed to as many other participants as possible.

A culture of teamwork in any endeavor will produce greater results than if one acted alone. In our lives, each of us is part of some group(s) seeking meaning through a community of like interests. Belonging to one or more is part of human nature.

In a different context but with its concept relative to meetings, consider how, in this example, a feeling of community among individuals resulted in a bonding and support among them to achieve common goals. In New York City, apartment building owners wanted to develop a communal sense even within the four walls of their buildings. They felt it would help to insure a positive relationship with tenants. They installed social rooms, a private exercise facility, showed movies, held concerts. The owners pointed out "We want to foster neighborly connections in an urban setting and instill a sense of cohesiveness among neighbors. When you know your neighbors, you're likely to be more respectful of them". Even here, in a totally different setting, through ingraining a feeling of community, the concept works.

Beyond program planning and the meeting design, those who plan programs should consider how greater meeting productivity could be achieved through the use of a facility, which contributes to a spirit of a community of people with like interests. It is in such a community that a fresh dimension toward gaining new knowledge can occur while culminating in an enjoyable learning experience for attendees, administrators and the meeting leadership.

An important additional advantage in attaining closeness among a group's participants is the likelihood that, after the session is over, individuals will continue to maintain contact. In doing so, they can discuss problems of implementation and ways of adapting the ideas generated in the meeting. Also, it will build new relationships and business networks.

4

The Psychological Factor in Meetings

It is important to recognize that there are psychological considerations in adult learning that have dramatic affect on achieving program goals and on an individual's learning process. Though these psychological factors may be subtle and subconscious, they nevertheless impact an individual's feeling of comfort and of learning readiness. These factors are embedded in an attendee's psyche from the moment she/he enters the meeting facility. They color the person's expectations of what to experience in the program. An attendee's state of mind in a meeting is an important factor in the participant's predisposition to learn.

The environment of a meeting facility can help the individual to move away, in a psychological sense, from thinking of the pressures of modern life, laying aside for the moment the fears, worries, frustrations not only of business but the problems at home. To the degree that organizations are unable to transform the mood and attitude away from those distractive thoughts, they will not be successful in attaining the total concentration required on the program subjects.

Emanuel Douchin made this observation from his research as Director of the Laboratory For Cognitive/Psycho Physiology at the University of Chicago. "Psychology is finding in the wake of new and compelling evidence that the unconscious mind may understand meanings, form emotional responses that, in turn, guide our behavior independent of conscious awareness".

Other research at The University of Chicago examined what happens when a person's mind is totally absorbed. It results in a condition called a "flow state". In such a state, their research indicates people experience greater motivation, deeper concentration and a "feeling" that they can reach a higher level of learning. The research concluded with this thought: learning and flow states will be achieved in an environment totally designed to enhance a positive attitude toward learning.

The late Dr. Harold Proshansky, who was dean of NYU's Graduate School, evolved a field called "environmental psychology". This concept underlines the importance of how all the factors in an environment will influence a person's attitude and actions. That philosophy has great relevance for examining how the many details in a meeting facility can either add or subtract from the attitude of attendees to achieve the meeting's objectives.

An entire issue of The New York Times magazine was devoted to the architectural design of structures. One was the design of a high school. The outside was striking. The interior, however, drew comments from students such as these: "This place feels a like a prison". "Why must all the walls be painted in greys. It's depressing. Aren't there brighter, happier colors that could be used"? Too often, reactions like these result from not devoting sufficient attention to the many details of the interior spaces of a school that affect the mood and attitude of the students and ultimately to the spirit in which they approach their learning.

Although not meeting environments, consider how the following different sites successfully achieve a psychological adjustment in people. Disney World was one of the most carefully researched and designed

places in the world. Management wanted visitors to feel, psychologically, that they had been transported into a "magic kingdom". There
were such names created as Frontierland, Fantasyland, Fairyland. The
details involved in the broad avenues, lights, colors, costumes, plants
were all integrated into a seamless environment that, they hoped,
would keep everyone in a state of euphoria. In doing so, they also
wanted adults to feel like a kid again bringing the family back for
another trip.

Consider further, as examples, how details in the design of these other
locations create a psychological affect on individuals:

Environment	Desired feeling/mood	Details that contribute to achievement of the desired effect
1. Disco	Excitement, participation, noise, movement, assault on all senses	Flashing lights, moving pictures, music with a loud beat, colorful decor, incense
2.Concert hall	Concentration, comfort, awe, respect, contemplation	Excellent acoustics, rich under-stated décor, subtle lighting, com-fortable seating, imposing proscenium, good sight lines
3.Church	Reverence, quietness,	Soft organ music, stained glass windows, expansive and elabo-rate ceilings, sculpture, pictures, refined décor

Although the intent of these places differs, there is a common concept
which has relevance for meetings: to eliminate outside influences which
interfere with their primary purpose: complete absorption, psychologically, of each person in the ultimate goals of these programs.

On the other hand, there can be an environment which has a negative
psychological impact on participants and its resultant effect on a meeting's outcome. Consider the potential problems in a facility such as

occurred in the following venue. An executive had a sales meeting of his staff in a former monastery, now a meeting place. He said it was the most unproductive meeting he had had with this group. His subsequent analysis determined that the architecture, stained glass windows, chapel and stone psychologically "spoke" of piety, spiritual serenity, contemplation. He observed participants were more subdued, quieter, more serious with less heated give and take than in previous meetings. One participant felt it was sacrilegious to hold a meeting here.

In another case, the University of McGill conducted an experiment. For two entire days, they had students study in a sterile, homogenous, unvarying environment. At the end of the two days, most could not endure it. They became bored, restless, and unable to concentrate.

Beyond these observations and experiments, there are lessons to be learned about the environment for meetings. For, there are significant psychological interrelationships and impacts that every space and detail in a facility can have on a participant's readiness to learn.

From the moment an attendee enters a meeting facility you want it to "say" you are being transformed into a different world. The environment should be warm, pleasant, calming, attractive, pressure free, inviting, different from the office environment. That feeling should be sustained throughout the entire meeting day, providing the participants that total immersion-learning environment. If meals are taken in the Company cafeteria, we are interrupting that adjustment by returning attendees back to their work setting. Or, for lunch, asking individuals to go to an outside, public restaurant brings them back to city life of noise, crowds, jostling, hardly an environment for interactions and learning.

Here are a few of the ways a facility can prepare and sustain positive attendee's feelings, mood and attitude.

1. As soon as a person enters the reception area, consider these details:

    a. The sound system plays quiet, light music

    b. Utilizing the positive findings of aromatherapy, a pleasant fragrance is sprayed

    c. The entry area should not remind one of an office reception room. Use an arrangement of furniture in a team set-up, as used in training programs, with seating of four in comfortable lounge chairs and a cube of a table.

    d. Add wall mirrors, plants, wall trimmings, and flowers.

    e. Staff members should be present to greet the participants and direct them to their meeting rooms. Attendees should sense a feeling of welcome in these new surroundings as soon as they arrive.

2. In the reception area use a specially designed desk that does not look like an office desk but rather is a decorative addition. Place pictures on the walls. The directory board should have a "welcome to participants" sign with a listing of all groups and the rooms assigned.

3. At the table where each attendee will sit in the meeting room, put out an attractive special orientation form. Because the facility will be new to many, this orientation helps every individual become familiar and comfortable with the facility and its services: location of rest rooms, how to get and send messages, location of break and lunch area, how to arrange transportation to airport, how to get and send faxes or duplicate material.

4. The lounge area should overlook a tranquil setting, giving participants an opportunity to look out on a relaxing and different environment from the meeting room. It is in such a setting that attendees are encouraged and feel comfortable to engage in informal interchanges, reviewing and adding to discussions.

5. Colors, comfortable seating, room shape, ceiling height and lighting are all to be researched and incorporated for their psychological influence on participant learning.

These details are a few of the considerations that should be weighed in considering how to optimize a participant's involvement in a meeting. But individual after individual remark how gracious, warm and pleasing they feel throughout the activities of a program as a result of these details.

These psychological elements, subtle but importantly, enhance the educational purpose of a meeting place. Psychological and physical comforts are prerequisite to mental alertness. The areas pointed out in this chapter are indicative of how an emphasis on and consideration of the psychological factors in a meeting can make a real difference in its outcome.

Spinoza was one of the 17th century monumental philosophers. His concepts still resonate today. In his masterwork book, The Ethics, he pointed out that reason is shot through with emotion. The critical role of emotion allows us to think. Spinoza then points out that feelings are not the enemy of reason but an indispensable accomplice. And so, we should weigh how our programs will benefit by considering ways in which the psychological dimension in a meeting can contribute not only to a sense of pride by meeting attendees in the choice of that facility, but also, in the end, to a heightened learning experience.

During a meeting at The Coleman Center, the following comment, with its psychological implications, was made by an executive attending a meeting of 60 of the associates from her company. "There's something magic in the air here".

In the chapter on Music, Colors, Lighting, Aroma, there is further coverage of psychological factors that resonate on meeting participants.

5

The Importance of Service in a Meeting Facility

Jack Welsh, former president of General Electric, when asked about reasons for GE's success, observed, "We produce great people who produce great products and <u>services</u>".

Client service is the ultimate imperative in a meeting facility. It is the sine qua non of any business. The staff must be flexible, informed, articulate, gracious, sensitive, quickly and professionally responsive to all enquires. They must equally meet the needs of both the attendees and the client leadership or administrator. It is important for the meeting facility to identify points of client contact, to have a clearly documented set of procedures to follow in those contacts and to regularly and continually provide staff training to assure that quality service is always rendered. These are the ingredients for a facility that will be recognized as a client oriented Center.

The services provided throughout the meetings' duration will create the critical positive impression of a center. Many opportunities for client contact happen even before the program begins. The following is a list some of these potential contacts:

Phone Services:

1. The manner in which the phone is answered and the accuracy of information that is provided by the staff member are impor-

tant factors in initial service implementation. Personal interface is far more essential than an automated system of
providing information. Rather than merely reciting the name
of the firm in a routine manner, the pleasant tone and rhythm
of the human voice immediately establishes an inviting
impression. Training to provide a high quality of phone contact is available from many sources. Answering the phone on
the first ring, and no more than three rings, provides a busi-
ness-like and professional impression for the caller. The person
answering the phone is more than a switchboard operator. He/
she must be oriented and trained to answer in a gracious manner any of the many questions or requests that will arise.
Equally important, if a question cannot be answered by the
staff member answering the call, there must be a procedure
established so that an answer, now or later, is provided to the
caller.

2. Initial Facility Tour:
    A critical contact occurs when visitors come to a facility for a
    tour. Their favorable impressions of service start with the man-
    ner in which the receptionist greets them. The receptionist
    should be trained not only to welcome them warmly but to ask
    for their names and business cards, take coats, offer a beverage
    and secure a staff member to give the tour. The staff giving the
    tour must also be oriented to greeting visitors graciously. They
    should be thoroughly familiar with the procedures for an
    informative tour, be completely knowledgeable about the
    facility's operation. He/she needs also to know what questions
    to ask, soliciting information and be aware of the material to
    give the visitor when leaving.

3. Answering the phone:
    When a phone caller inquires about a meeting, the member of
    the sales staff, that takes the call, should know the name of the
    person calling. That information results from the receptionist

obtaining the name and organization of the caller and having passed the information on to the sales person. So, when the sales staff answers with "good morning" or "good afternoon" with the person's name, there is a positive familiarity established. The sales staff asks a series of questions previously prepared to ascertain the needs of the prospect. Another service point has been passed.

4. Contract Signing:

    When a contract has been signed, another service kicks in. A staff member will be in touch with the meeting planner. A series of additional prepared questions, asked of the planner, determines every need of the meeting. In many cases, this procedure will often lead the planner to determine details not originally considered. These facts are reviewed with appropriate staff in a meeting one week prior to the client program. In that meeting, questions are answered and procedures clarified. In this manner, all of the requirements of a meeting are understood, anticipated, and prepared for by all personnel who will be in contact with attendees and leaders. No surprises should occur at the meeting itself. Every detail has at this point anticipated thus making unnecessary multiple calls to the meeting planner.

5. Meeting Interface Procedure:

    Another important contact is made at the meeting itself. Before the program begins, a member of the facility staff meets with the leader of the meeting in the room of the program. At that point, the staff reviews all of the pre-determined specifications of the meeting, and makes any changes desired. At the same time, an orientation is given of the room: light controls, air conditioning switches, A-V operation and how to call if additional help is required. Throughout the meeting, the facility staff checks with the leader to determine whether any further help is needed.

6. Staff Location:
    Staff offices should be spread around the Center, not concentrated in one place. Thus, it is easier for anyone to locate a staff member when assistance is needed. Career clothes for woman and special, identifiable clothes for men will facilitate an attendee's ability to question or seek help from staff.

Not one of the services mentioned should stand-alone nor are they intended to be all-inclusive. However, they are illustrative. There will be other points of contact at which the service equation must be implemented. Service is a critical adjunct to and soul of the smooth and efficient operation of a meeting facility. Its cumulative impact will provide, if consciously carried out, an overwhelmingly favorable impression of this special learning environment. The most important source of competitive advantage for any organization comes from its people and the services they provide.

Note on the following pages a rating scale to measure the services provided in a meeting facility that one may use.

Measuring The Quality of the Service In A Meeting Facility

The factors following identify the areas of a facility in which service is important for the needs of the leaders, attendees, and administrator of your meeting. As you study each of these service factors, circle, on the right, the qualitative number to which you believe that facility has met your requirements. Then, add up the circled numbers and insert that number in the space provided. Then compare your rating to the standards on page 30.

Service Factor	Rating (Circle one number for each factor)
A. Is facility staff readily accessible and located on the same floor as your meeting?	0 1 2 3 4
B. Is a trained staff member on hand to handle questions or solve problems regarding A-V equipment and technology?	0 1 2 3 4
C. How quickly responsive is the staff to your request for assistance?	0 1 2 3 4
D. How pleasant and gracious do you find the attitude of the facility staff in working with them?	0 1 2 3 4
E. Have requests of attendees been handled promptly, efficiently and with grace?	0 1 2 3 4
F. How knowledgeable was the staff in answering questions?	0 1 2 3 4
G. Were your meeting rooms cleaned and serviced throughout the meeting day?	0 1 2 3 4
H. Throughout the meeting, does the staff, on its own, take the initiative to check with the leadership on their needs?	0 1 2 3 4
I. How easy and accessible is it to send and receive faxes, duplicate material, make transparencies, arrange transportation?	0 1 2 3 4
J. On your arrival, was the set-up of your program and materials put out exactly the ways you had asked prior to your meeting?	0 1 2 3 4

Add Your Total _____

Qualitative Rating Values

Enter here your total from the previous page_____

Quality	Rating	Check here (√) which of your total above falls within which category
Excellent	37-40	_____
Very Good	33-36	_____
Good	29-32	_____
Fair	25-28	_____
Poor	Below 24	_____

This rating will serve as a guide as to how well the meeting facility measures up in terms of the service provided for your program.

6

Decisions That Limit A Facility's Effectiveness As A Learning Center

The National Association of Program Instruction devoted an entire issue to the subject of the meeting environment. The following statements were made: "It became apparent that there were many people who wanted information on learning environment design. There was a notable lack of resources from which to draw and a lack of facilities to write about. There seems to be an abundance of pretty buildings, but few that can be said to blend what we know of learning theory and architectural creativity. Until all parts of the process are given equal consideration, that is, a systematic approach to instruction and the improvement of the learning environment, all must recognize that we are only doing part of our job." It is important to identify and to eliminate all negative factors that may interfere with the primary function of a meeting facility to contribute to greater meeting results. They include such considerations as the following:

1. Underestimating the complexities and nuances crucial for an effective learning center.

   A facility chosen for an organization's meetings is a statement by management which represents the value that management places not only on learning, education and training, but also the importance it attaches to the personnel attending the programs. In choosing a quality center, consideration must be first given to the interactions of the individual with the meeting environment, examining how all the spaces in the center can enhance the participant's activities-interaction during discussions, networking with other attendees, relaxation, study and note-taking. It must be examined as an environment that caters to all the daily activities of the participant. If a simplistic approach is taken to the role of a meeting Center, essentially just providing space, then the full potential of the meeting objectives will not be met. Understanding the role, purpose and concept of a learning-engineered facility is critical if it is to be the active ingredient it can be for more productive meetings. These objectives require a deeper knowledge of learning theory, environmental psychology, trade craft, strobe hypnosis, human factors engineering and similar thinking so that the planner and designer of a learning center can relate them to that specialized and unique task.

2. Providing architects and interior designers the initial responsibility for defining the parameters of the meeting facility.

The architect and interior designer are obviously vital to the ultimate success of a facility. However, their important contributions should be made in an appropriate sequence. First, the detailed specifications of a meeting center should start with the input of a staff steeped in and knowledgeable of both the processes of learning as well as the demands they impose on meeting attendees. Within that framework, subsequent steps can then be taken. These steps involve preparing specifications of the many details to be included and what you want them to achieve such as ceiling height, wall color, HVAC, door placement, dimensions and purposes of various rooms and their position relative to each other followed by a suggested layout. These are not engineering specifications but a road map and a statement of the facility's goals and the end results to be achieved. This guidance provides a direction for the other professionals to follow, without in any way, inhibiting subsequent creativity and innovativeness. The same process and concept are employed in the design of a golf course. Those who have played and understand the game, like Jack Nicklaus, first establish the initial requirements of the course-the number of holes, the traps, the rough, distances, the layout. Then the landscape architects can take over and, using those guideline to then design the course.

3. Incorporation of advanced, sophisticated audio-visual technology and systems.

Video-conferencing, E-learning, web casting, and other advanced technological developments have proven their value as components of a communications and educational strategy. However, it may prove to be an excessive investment to automatically include in a meeting center and its' rooms all of these technological tools. Recognize that in practice, program leaders generally find it is effective and comfortable to employ the more basic tools: multi-media and overhead projectors, chart pads and broad band wiring, internet access for computers. One factor for the reluctance of some leaders to use more complicated systems may be because leaders are not yet comfortable with these technological capabilities. However, there is a fundamental customer premise here: "Give the customer what they want, not what you think they should have"

4. Reexamining approaches for researching the needs of a facility.

Here are typical approaches taken to establish the facility footprint and their potential flaws:

A. As part of the study on meeting environments conducted by The National Association of Program Instruction the following statement was made: "It should hardly surprise any of us to know that only a handful of educational and training facilities have been designed scientifically with the same systematic care we are increasingly giving to course development". Thus, in visiting other facilities looking for new ideas and guidance, one could be perpetuating the mistakes or lack of forward vision that others have incorporated in their center. Here is an approach that might help to provide some useful thoughts. Ask the center director of the facility you are visiting this question: "If you were able to start the planning of this facility from its' very beginning, what changes would you now make?"

B. Using a committee or appointing a company person to work on the project. The experience and specialized knowledge crucial in the initial planning and design, before the architect's input, are typically missing from these groups. Their resulting report may lack the forward thinking concepts and ideas necessary for the participant's total immersion in a new environment. It is one that will not only contribute to learning, but to attendee's enjoyment while also supporting the program leaders so that they can more effectively communicate and guide discussions. The company personnel, working on this project, may be able to serve best as a program manager rather than the facility visionaries.

C. Sending a questionnaire to potential users. A well designed questionnaire can be helpful in determining user needs such as: the number of programs held, the number of attendees, A-V requirements, and the set-up required. But, to ask respondents for substantial answers on facility design from a learning standpoint may produce little of value. Also, though willing to be helpful, their answers are given hastily.

5. Continuing to reinforce the primary purpose of the facility as a learning force not concentrating only on its aesthetics.
Beauty and function are compatible. There is not a basic conflict between a structure that is striking in appearance and one of learning effectiveness. However, the initial start begins by establishing the functions and specifications that will maximize the absorption of information by attendees and add to the performance of program leadership. Then, within these parameters, the prestige building with the striking interiors can be created.

6. Adapting as meeting rooms those spaces primarily designed for social functions.
Space may be provided in these rooms but they are counter-productive to provide an environment that enhances concentration and will reduce participant fatigue. Some of the inadequacies include the following: poor lighting that tires eyes; distractive wall hangings or overly decorative wallpaper; uncomfortable seating; poor noise control; rooms oversized that "lose" the smaller number of participants; not conducive for A-V use. It is

essential that such rooms are avoided for successful meeting results.

7. Keeping all the activities of the meeting within one facility.

A psychological and mental transformation must occur when an individual enters the special environment of a meeting Center. The aesthetics and spaces of the facility should promote a change in thinking of the activist and doer to a mind set that induces relaxation, quiet and reduced feeling of pressure. These adjustments are prerequisite for heightened learning, concentration, participation, listing and interaction. If participants move to other sites for program activities, those changes are counter-productive to the initial, positive immersion in the principal meeting center. Such changes can take place if breaks are taken in a corridor where people are passing through or meals are taken in either the company cafeteria or in outside restaurants. The process then of reentry into the principal meeting place results in a subtle but unnecessary readjustment back to the familiar and primary learning environment.

7

The Conference Room as a Critical Factor in Meeting Success: It Must Be Far More Than Just Space

The room in which a group primarily meets should be given special attention. It is the springboard for information accumulation and participant discussion.

The design criteria for a conference room is unique, with limited, if any relationship to those for a residence or an office. It is important to recognize those important differences if the room is to achieve its primary function, which is to serve as a positive contributor for more productive meetings. Too often, the room is thought of as merely providing "space". The primary objectives and contributions of a learning effective conference room environment should be: to maximize participant's absorption of and concentration on the information presented, to facilitate the flow and interchange of this information among participants and to support the meeting leadership in communicating information and guiding discussions.

The typical conference room is most often designed for groups of between 10-50 persons and is optimized for meetings of a day or longer rather than the 30 minutes to an hour get-together. The more frequent use is for programs other than Board meetings, which have special requirements.

Michelangelo wrote, "Perfection is made of trifles." In a conference room, perfection is made of the meticulous attention to tens of details (trifles) though each of itself may seem minor. Here are some of those details to be considered in a conference room that can contribute to enhancing and optimizing participant learning. Though details should not be obvious to the participant but each has a profound affect on the comfort and psychology of an individual, thereby adding to mental alertness.

1. **Conference Room Shape**

   A square room will bring people more closely together. In doing so, it is far easier to see, as well as hear and also feel a part of a community with common interests.People in a long, narrow room are separated from front to rear. That separation is counter to encouraging participant inter-change and a feeling of group unity. Also the remoteness makes it harder for those in the rear to identify with the leadership in front. The length of a room should not exceed its width by more than 50% i.e. 20'w X 30'l, maximum.

   Place doors in the rear of the room. If placed in front, it is distractive when attendees, for personal reasons, leave the room, walking past the leader while the meeting is still in progress. Use doors also that open and close quietly.

2. **Lighting**

   People underestimate the power of light; it can lift our spirits or conversely make a person feel downcast. "Light therapy" is a remarkable new field of research and treatment for improving moods through the proper use of light sources and types.

Lighting engineers describe a condition they call "strobe hypnosis"—it refers to the ways in which fatigue is induced among individuals through "strobes" of light striking their eyes over a period of time. These phenomena can occur as the result of the improper placement of light fixtures, the intensity of the light or its "color".To the degree that these light reflections continuously strike participants' eyes they will, eventually, reduce concentration. The blue-white fluorescents, which are typically used, casts a pale look on faces and colors while its stronger rays will, in time, induce eye weariness ("hypnosis"). Cove lighting produces a strong band of light on the top of walls creating undesirable shadows beneath. Side fixtures, though pretty, are distractive. Knowledgeable lighting designers can be of great help in overcoming these challenges.

There is a new advance in fluorescents that throws a softer, more pleasing and natural light, though of ample lumen at table height. It is far more "comfortable" and easier on the eyes.

Various controls for different banks of light are a plus. When projection is used, the banks of lights over the screen should be turned off for easier viewing of projected material. Dimmers are necessary when projected material is employed.

3. **Wall Color**

The late Faber Birren was the country's foremost authority on colors. His research underlined the psychological impact of various colors on people. In a meeting room, wall colors of white or ivory, though appropriate for a residence, are not desirable because of the eye glare they induce. Greys connote depressing thoughts (as in a grey day). Colors can project sadness, melancholia, happiness, relaxation and memories of past events. The meeting room colors should connote calmness and relaxation. Mr. Birren's research shows that the colors that will induce pleasant sensations are blue, yellow, green or orange.

4. **Ceilings**
   Ceiling height should be at least 9' preferably closer to 10'. Lower ceilings give an uncomfortable feeling of being compressed. The height of the ceiling is also a critical parameter for determining the placement of projection equipment as well as the type of sound proofing to include.

5. **Furniture**
   a. Chairs
      Stack chairs are poor for individual comfort. Chairs should incorporate these features: five wheels, swivel, arms, reclining back, soft seat, adjustments for height and back tension, with non-slip material of pleasant colors on seat and back.

   b. Tables
      Tabletops should have a soft look, perhaps light leather, but not white shades. Each person should have a minimum of 2 ½' of horizontal space. Its width is desirably 2 feet minimum. Use a modesty panel to avoid the distraction of people crossing and uncrossing legs.

6. **Screens**
   They should be recessed in the ceiling, automatically raised when not in use. Participants should not have to

stare continuously at a white surface when the screen is lowered but not needed. The screen needs to be of the highest quality to minimize viewing distortion. The size of the screen should follow those standards specified to meet the usual requirements of participants as a factor of room size.

7. **Use of Computers**

    A number of programs employ computers as part of the meeting design. To avoid the exposure of dangling wires, consider these additions: use tables that have a compartment in front for electrical, communication and convection for wires. Also, place electrical outlets in the floor or in the walls throughout the room into which plugs can be inserted. Ensure that there are sufficient electrical and communication jacks in front of the room.

8. **A Lounge**

    Near the meeting room, in a separate space, create a lounge. Throughout the meeting and at breaks, attendees can come here, in a different environment, to have snacks, soft drinks, coffee, tea, fruit. Set up seating for 4, 5 and 8 where individuals can gather and sit informally to discuss topics related to the program. Try to place the lounge in an area overlooking the outdoors.

9. **Distractions to avoid**

    a. Paintings, pictures, photographs placed on the meeting room walls, while decorative, will cause participants, in studying them, to take their minds off discussions, even if only momentarily. Do not place them in the conference room but rather place them in the lounge.

b. Eliminate noises from such sources as air-conditioning, corridors, adjacent rooms and outside traffic.

c. White writing surfaces reflect lights and can become a source of fatigue over time.

d. If there is poor temperature control, it will affect concentration.

10. **<u>Aids for the Leadership</u>**

Consideration should be given to ways to reduce their fatigue and to assist the leadership to concentrate on their primary duties: communicating information, guiding discussion.

a. Leadership special chair

As leaders stand in front of their groups for extended periods, they become leg weary. To reduce that fatigue, leaders will sit on the edge of a table or sit in the same chair as attendees, and, in doing so, lose that psychological presence as the "authority" figure. Use a special chair with these features: its' height is that of a bar stool so that the leader can see over the heads of the group, it has wheels, arms, back, a pedestal for legs to rest and an adjustable height.

b. System for hanging chart pad paper

As the meeting progresses and information is written on chart pads, the paper is torn off and spread on the walls in the room. The typical approach is to tear off pieces of masking tape and place it against the wall. The resulting look of papers is one of disorganization. One solution that has been developed has resulted in a far easier procedure for the leaders while presenting a more organized appearance to the sheets of paper spread throughout the room.

The system consists of a line of one inch metal strips. Attached to the strips are several three inches magnets with a knob handle. The leader readily places a paper on the strip, putting a magnet at each end. The result is information organized, in a straight line, visually pleasing.

c. Supply cabinet

Throughout a meeting, the leader may need additional pens, writing pads, whiteouts, a three-hole punch, paper clips, stapler and other materials. Rather than having to scurry around for these supplies, a small wooden 5 door cabinet should be placed in the corner in front of the room. As needed, the leader can readily secure supplies.

d. Outlet for projection equipment

Rather than tripping over wires to the projection equipment, an outlet 8' from the wall will facilitate the plugging in of equipment with wires out of the way.

11. **Acoustics**

An acoustical expert should be consulted to assure the room is properly sound proofed to eliminate echoes and "quiet" spots.

Some conference rooms are highly sophisticated technological centers. For their needs, they incorporate interactive audio, video, data transmission along with a system for receiving information and pictures. But, the more typical needs for most meetings use these aids: data projector, VCR, TV, DVD unit, overhead projector, microphone, T-1 or other high speed line, floor and wall wiring, hook-up for computers, computer monitors or plasma screen.

The Wall Street Journal had an article titled "Button—Down Conference Rooms Loosen Up". The article describes the approach taken by several planners to design conference rooms that they hoped will loosen up participants and, presumably, will contribute ultimately to more productive meetings. The following are examples of such conference rooms these planners have suggested. Consider whether you would like to hold a meeting in one of these rooms.

1. This "room" has no walls. It has an alcove with cocktail lounge seating and a full kitchen adjacent where participants can go throughout the meeting to prepare refreshments.

2. This room has a basketball hoop with half-court markings on the hardwood floor.

3. One conference room has overstuffed chairs with a swivel arm on which participants can rest pads for note taking. There are no tables.

4. This conference room has a canoe dangling from the ceiling. Its presence is intended to give attendees the feeling of being out-doors.

5. A room that has glass walls shaped into a semi-circle.

One can judge whether any of the five rooms outlined above would serve the needs of a learning oriented environment.

The conference room with features described in the foregoing pages will not only contribute to participant learning and enjoyment but, as important, to leadership performance. Create an "educational" oasis. In doing so, this specially designed space will add an extra dimension to the success of a meeting.

8

Measuring The Learning Effectiveness of a Meeting Facility

A critical element in the success of a meeting is the quality of the facility in which a program is held. In the case of a company owned center, the selection of a site may be pre-ordained. In selecting an outside facility, the choice is made often through either a site inspection or some one's recommendation.

Whether a company meeting facility or an outside location, it would be prudent to step back to determine the relative value of the critical elements of the options offered by a meeting facility. In doing so, one can ascertain, in a quantifiable manner the potential worth of a meeting facility in terms of its cost, time loss by participants from work, its effort to plan and execute the program and the impact on attendees.

The guide that has been developed looks at and offers numerical measurements in three areas of a facility: the principal meeting room, the breakout room and the area for breaks.

The checklists that follow are based on studies of attendees, meeting design and procedures for hundreds of small group meetings. Consider the factors in each of these three environments. On the right of the checklist, there is a rating scale for each environment. Think carefully about each, circling the value you would grade for each. The higher the number you check, the higher the rating. Then, total the ratings selected and enter that number in the space at the bottom of each scale. When you've completed your additions, measure your totals for each of the three environments against the provided scale that defines the standards for the three areas. These rated factors, though they may not be all-inclusive, will help to focus on areas that may not be immediately apparent. However, they do influence the ways in which a meeting participant interacts with others, concentrates, relaxes, studies, thinks and ultimately not only learns but also enjoys the experience in that program.

I. Principal Meeting Room Environment	RATING (circle one number) Low High
A.	The room is square or slightly rectangle. Not long and narrow whereby the participants in the rear are removed from the other participants and the leader.	0 1 2 3 4
B.	Lighting is evenly spread throughout the room. No spots of light. No high and low shadows on walls. No sconces, chandelier or cove lighting	0 1 2 3 4
C.	No reflective surfaces from mirrors, glass, TV monitors, crystal, chrome. Reflections will cause eye fatigue and reduce perceptual levels	0 1 2 3 4
D.	Wall colors of bright shades of such colors as blue, orange, yellow, green. Not whites, browns, blacks which are depressing after long exposure, or bright reds or similar loud colors, plaids or stripes which are distracting	0 1 2 3 4
E.	Rugs throughout the facility are solid colors. No plaids or stripes which are fatiguing to the eye after extended exposure	0 1 2 3 4
F.	Ceiling at least 9', preferably close to 10'. Avoid feeling of compression. Low ceilings are difficult for projection	0 1 2 3 4
G.	Chairs with arms, swivel, wheels and reclining back, covered with attractive, subdued material	0 1 2 3 4
H.	Tables that provide 2 ½' between participants with modesty panel on table. Rich looking top requiring no covering and hard enough to write on	0 1 2 3 4
I.	No pictures, sculpture pieces, art, clocks on wall, which even momentarily, will lead participants to study taking mind off discussion.	0 1 2 3 4
J.	Light controls on front wall operable by the meeting leader. Dimmers in room.	0 1 2 3 4
K.	Audiovisual controls at front with leader able to operate easily.	0 1 2 3 4

L.	Air-conditioning and heating controls in room. Quiet system with good ventilation capabilities.	0 1 2 3 4
M.	Incorporation and availability of newest communication technology and wiring.	0 1 2 3 4
N.	Comfortably sized for number of people in groups	0 1 2 3 4

Your Total_____

II. Break-Out Room Environment	RATING (circle one number) Low High
A. Room appropriately sized for number in your group. Not too large or small with ceiling height at least 9', preferably close to 10'. Avoid feeling of compression. Difficult for projection. Note "F" on meeting room criteria.	0 1 2 3 4
B. Room specially designed for small meetings. Not a 'make-do' room. Tables that provide 2 ½' between participants with modesty panel on table. Rich looking top requiring no covering and hard enough to write on. Note "H" previously.	0 1 2 3 4
C. Chairs with arms, swivel, wheels and reclining back, covered with attractive, subdued material. Note "G" previously.	0 1 2 3 4
D. Lighting is evenly spread throughout the room. No spots of light. No high and low shadows on walls. No sconces, chandelier or cove lighting. Note "B" previously.	0 1 2 3 4
E. Quiet area	0 1 2 3 4
F. Communication equipment installed with wiring for computer use. Note "M" previously.	0 1 2 3 4
G. Easy walking distance from principal meeting room	0 1 2 3 4

Your Total_____

III. Environment for Breaks and Informal Socializing	RATING (circle one number)
A. Separate area	0 1 2 3 4
B. Comfortable lounge seating in groupings of 4-8.	0 1 2 3 4
C. Range of light refreshments and beverages. Self-service and easy to obtain. Available throughout meeting.	0 1 2 3 4
D. Cheerful decor.	0 1 2 3 4
E. Quiet area	0 1 2 3 4
F. Area overlooks tranquil outdoor setting.	0 1 2 3 4
G. Subdued lighting. sconces, chandeliers possible here.	0 1 2 3 4

Your Total_____

RATING SCALES FOR THREE AREAS

Check your totals for each of three areas to the rating standards on the right side of this page. Compare your facility's evaluation.

I. Main Meeting Room

Enter your rating for your room

Quality

_____

a.	Excellent	50-56
b.	Very Good	44-49
c.	Good	39-43
d.	Fair	35-38
e.	Poor	Below 34

II. Break-out Room

Enter your rating for your room

Quality

_____

a.	Excellent	23-24
b.	Very Good	20-22
c.	Good	18-19
d.	Fair	16-17
e.	Poor	Below 15

III. Breaks and Informal Socializing

Enter your rating for your room

Quality

_____

a.	Excellent	27-28
b.	Very Good	24-26
c.	Good	22-23
d.	Fair	19-21
e.	Poor	Below 18

9

Music, Colors, Lighting, Aroma—Their Impact on Learning

Though music, colors, lighting and aroma in a meeting environment have been briefly mentioned before, their discernible affect on attendee's comfort, attitude, fatigue reduction and learning readiness merits expansion and further study. Each of itself may not seem important, but their cumulative impact can provide significant positive reactions from participants. They are elements that, subtly, help to provide a learning environment.

Music

The impact of music in a meeting environment, when planned carefully, can be calming, arousing or pleasurable. Depending on the end result desired, the choice of musical pieces facilitates your goals. For example, Disneyland has created music in its various areas to induce calmness and heightened pleasurable experiences.

Carnegie Institute of Technology conducted an experiment testing the role of music in an architectural drafting room. The discovered that not only did the efficiency of the work of the drafting room improve but employee speed as well.

Moods can be impacted through various kinds of music, selected for different purposes during a meeting, such as the following:

1. To lift the spirits of a group and convey the feeling that they are entering a different environment than their work setting, play, as example, the following music as attendees enter the reception and registration area for the meeting.

    a. For example, Schubert's "Faith In Spring" or any of the preludes or mazurkas of Chopin.

2. Before the sessions begin in the principal meeting room, consider the use of soaring type of music.

    a. For example, Gershwin's "Rhapsody In Blue" or Sousa's "Stars and Stripes Forever".

3. In the break area or at the end of the day, try calming pieces with an easy rhythm style.

    a. For example, Debussy's "Claire de Lune" or Dvorak's New World Symphony", Strauss's "Blue Danube Waltz".

Though individuals may not be consciously aware of the music, if you want to check on its effectiveness, ask participants, at the end of a meeting, their impressions of its positive or negative affect. One might be surprised at their favorable comments when the presence of this music is consciously brought to participant's attention. Gerald Zaltman, professor at Harvard, wrote the book How Customers Think. From his research with many companies, Mr. Zaltman observed that 95% of the thinking that drives individual behavior occurs subconsciously. Music, appropriately used, underlines that observation.

AROMA

The field of aromatherapy has received extensive study and examination of test results by scientists. They have discovered that the sense of smell is the only one of our senses that reacts directly on our brain. The

Fragrance Foundation's research found that the sense of smell is one of the body's most potent barometers. The brain responds to odors with pleasure, emotion and creativity.

The scientists at the University of Cincinnati assembled two groups, each to complete the same tasks. One group breathed normal air. The individuals in the second group were treated with scented air. The results were striking. The latter group performed much better than the former group. Once again, though this factor in a meeting group may be subconscious, its' cumulative affect will create positive attitudes toward the learning experience. For example:

1. In the reception and registration area, a pleasant light fragrance will immediately permeate the attendee's sense of smell, providing an experience suggesting they are entering a different environment of relaxation, quiet, pressure-free.

2. In the meeting room at breaks, spraying a woodsy smell may be appreciated. As one leader expressed when returning to the meeting room, sensing a difference, "What a clean smell in the air. It can't be just the air-conditioning".

3. In the rest rooms, particularly, a mild fragrance is a pleasant welcome. The late famous anthropologist, Margaret Mead said, "You can never have a relationship with someone whose smell you don't like". That thought might be imaginatively extrapolated for the "smell" of a meeting facility.

COLORS

Scientists and psychologists recognize that color values evoke psychological responses and moods in people. These responses to color can range from warmth to coolness or tranquility. The late Faber Birren was considered the world's foremost authority on the influence that colors have on individuals. In his famous book, Psychological Implications of Color, he wrote, "Color affects muscular tension, brain waves, heart rates, respiration and other functions of our automatic nervous system. These conditions, in turn, arouse emotional and aesthetic reactions, likes and dislikes, pleasant and unpleasant associations". In support of these observations, a pioneer in biofeedback research, Barbara Brown wrote in her book, New Mind New Body, "Color induces emotional states which are specific to different hues i.e. brain electrical response to red is alerting, arousal; to blue it is relaxation".

The selection of colors in a meeting facility's rooms, break area, lunch room, reception, offices, are indeed, a factor of what that color is intended to convey to a participant's psyche, brain, emotions, and ultimately, to the productivity of the meeting.

In the selection of colors in a Conference Center, typically the choices have followed the rationale of the ones used in offices or homes. While appropriate for these settings, whites, greys, ivories and crèmes are, in a meeting, colors that induce either fatigue over extended exposure or promote drab feelings.

Hospitals are discovering, too, that the colors formerly used in patient rooms and corridors were de-spiriting. They have now found that using colors like blue and green have helped to not only calm patients but also assisted patients to deal more effectively with pain. Leatrice Eisenman, executive director of the Pantene Color Institute, observed from her tests. "If one is surrounded by nothing but somber colors, their dullness makes an individual both fatigued and depressed". The selection of colors in a meeting facility should consider these feelings conveyed by different colors:

1. Restful, calming, tranquil

2. Impart a reminder of happy memories

3. Feeling of a sunny, pleasant day

4. Whites and greys project a feeling of sterility (as in a hospital room and should not be used)

A group of Munich psychologists called Gesellesschaft fur Rationelle Psychologies were studying the affect of colors on the behavior of school children. There were two control groups set up. One was placed in rooms painted in whites, browns, and greys. The second in rooms painted in blues and oranges. The results of the test were significant. Those in the second group were not only more alert but more creative. In addition to the stimulation of mental performance, the psychologists also observed an improvement in the social interaction among individuals. In a meeting facility, greater study of the use of colors is warranted for its potential affect on participant's sense of well-being, social interaction and greater attention to the material being communicated.

LIGHTING

Lighting is more than a convenience in a meeting room, deserving far more attention than the choice of a bulb and fixture. Relative little attention has been directed to the impact of lighting on mood, and in turn, on behavior and cognition. Scientific research has shown that lighting can indeed influence mood which may, then, influence thought and action. In P.R. Boyce McMillan's book Human Factors In Lighting, he points out, "Lighting contributes to people's impression of space. Lighting can give interior space a "character": dramatic, inviting, depressing, boring, relaxing, interesting, functional. These are factors to consider: the intensity of light; its glare; its color. These factors can create distractions away from concentration and induce fatigue from the glare".

Even as early as the 1920's, Western Electric was testing the factor of lighting. In the famous study conducted in its Hawthorne plant outside Chicago, they discovered that variations in light levels at employee's work place dramatically affected a worker's performance.

The lighting questions to be addressed in a meeting center are as follows:

1. How best should a meeting room be lit so that any projection of information is seen clearly without "bleeding" from the room's overhead light?

2. What lighting will provide a natural look to color and to the faces of attendees, eliminating the pale, ashen look of the wrong "color" of lights?

3. What lighting will create a restful, comfortable ambience for participants, negating elements that induce eye fatigue?

Here is a list of goals to be achieved in lighting a meeting room:

1. Place lighting controls on the instructional wall, easily accessible to the leader. Each switch clearly marked as to the light it controls.

2. At table height, provide 60-80 foot candles for the comfort and work of participants.

3. Walls of meeting rooms should be "washed" with 40-50 foot candles. Eliminate high and low shadows on wall. Cove lighting presents a harsh light of brightness on walls, fatiguing to participants.

4. When projecting visuals, use dimmers and turn off only the lights above the projection screen.

5. Light fixture lenses should be chosen to dispense light evenly.

6. Choose a fluorescent that projects "natural" light not the frequently used blue-white fluorescent that casts a pale look on the face of a participant.

7. Space the fixtures around the room so that there is an even dispersal of light.

The above suggestions relate to meeting rooms. Lighting in the lounge area for breaks or the area for meals should be more decorative, but equally as supportive of the facility's objective as a learning environment.

In essence, lighting establishes a mood. It influences our mental and psychological well-being. Lighting can impact how we absorb information, how it induces fatigue, how we perform our work. It deserves far more attention than merely providing illumination.

Music, colors, lighting, aroma are, together, important factors in the total panorama of a meeting facility. Each needs to be seriously recognized, for all four create a striking plus for heightened participant learning and comfort.

10

Measuring Participant Reactions to a Program

At the end of a program, participants are typically given a question-naire to determine the value that attendees attribute to a meeting. The series of questions have a rating to be applied to each. Often, the rat-ings are this type of evaluation: excellent, very good, good, fair and poor. While providing some indication of participant reactions, there are other approaches to get a closer approximation of what an attendee thinks. Here are some thoughts.

At the opening of the questionnaire, these instructions are suggested: Please rate each question on a scale of 1 to 10-10 being the highest rat-ing.

(Another approach could be)

To provide your answers to each of the following questions, please place a long, diagonal line at any point on this scale either on the lines or between them—10 is the highest rating

<table>
<tr><td>1</td><td>.</td><td>.</td><td>.</td><td>5</td><td>.</td><td>.</td><td>.</td><td>.</td><td>10</td></tr>
</table>

(If you use this scale, it needs to be placed after each question).

Here is a sample of questions you might ask.

1.   How effective was <u>(name of speaker or leader)</u> in communicating information that you found useful? Rating_____

Comments:

_____

_____

(If there is more than one speaker, an additional question(s) for each speaker should be included with that person's name in the above blank space)

2.   Following the talk of the above speaker, how participative and useful was the discussion time? Rating_____

Comments:

_____

_____

(If there are multiple speakers, follow question 1 for every other speaker)

3.   If visuals were used how informative were they and was the material easy to read and understandable? Rating_____

Comments:

_____

_____

4.   After each presentation, was there sufficient time allowed for the informal mingling with other participants and was the facility conducive to allow for this interaction? Rating_____

Comments:

_____

_____

5.   Do you believe the information gained in this meeting will have application in your work? Rating_____

Comments:

_____

_____

6. What is your reaction to this facility in terms of your easy accessibility to its spaces, responsiveness to your needs, pleasure within its environment and the services it provides? Rating_____

Comments:

_____

_____

Another way to gauge participant reactions to your program is to undertake this approach. Follow up with a telephone call to six or eight previous participants. Do so two weeks after the meeting. Ask the following types of questions:

1. Now that you are back at work, what, if any, ideas or information in the program have you found helpful?

2. Is there any of the material you learned that you have now put into use in your work?

3. What are your thoughts about how we might improve any aspect of our program so that it can be even more beneficial to future attendees?

This telephone approach could provide greater depth of information than is possible from the written questionnaire often answered in haste, as participants are anxious to get home.

A further follow-up contact could be made to speakers, asking their thoughts about ways to improve the meeting.

The numerical ratings and any comments included will provide actions to guide you in future programs:

1. If using the same speaker is an option, you can decide whether to invite that presenter in the future. If you will be using the same person, then give the speaker feedback with suggestions as to how a future participation can be improved

2. If your meeting is held in an outside facility, based on the evaluation, you can decide whether to hold other programs there. If an internal center, give feedback to the executive in charge of the facility.

3. The evaluations can help the program developers to make changes, if needed, in the design of the meeting.

Conclusion

Meetings will never be replaced as the singular forum for personal communication and interaction. A meeting blends individuals, emotionally and intellectually, into a group of interrelated and interdependent interests.

The preceding chapters have explored areas that need reemphasis and reexamination: the intrinsic nature of any meeting with its distinctive advantage as a learning medium; the psychological and community implications that occur in a meeting to be integrated in its planning; the details required within a facility that contribute to a program's success; the services to be provided to the leadership and to attendees enhancing their participation; measurement approaches to assess the program's impact on participants.

On the job, the thinking of an individual necessitates an immersion in the worries, problems and pressures of the work world. However, in a meeting, an attendee has a different role, entailing a psychological adjustment. Here, the participant is in a more passive mode. As such, she/he requires intense concentration, listening, probing, interacting no longer the activist and doer.

There is a great responsibility a planner assumes in the conception, development, organization and execution of a meeting. In total, these programs impact the brains of thousands of attendees positively or negatively.

The insights and thoughts in the preceding chapters are designed to invigorate the practices, planning and processes in the execution of a meeting and, in turn, aim to convert a meeting into a forum that has an optimal impact on attendees.

Further, through reading these pages, I hope you have gained fresh insights into how a meeting facility, focused on learning, will contribute to more productive programs. Inclusive, within that broader thinking, is a Center specially designed for small group meetings with a professional, responsive staff implementing client oriented procedures all of which have proven, at The Coleman Center, to result in a greater impact of learning for participants as well as an improved level of performance by the session's leadership.

The Coleman Center

The Coleman Center has built its brand name recognition and its national reputation around objectives and visions created to serve meeting clients with the highest standards:

1. Developing a special learning environment for a meeting that contributes to the participant's education and pleasure while assisting the client to achieve maximum results in his/her program.

2. Providing a professional, knowledgeable client-oriented and supportive staff who anticipates and responds immediately to every need of the clients—the leaders, administrators or participants.

3. Developing and implementing procedures designed to relieve a client of any facility-related problem so that the sessions can proceed most smoothly and productively.

In The New York Times article about the Coleman Center, the Center was described as "the perfect environment for meetings."

For further information, please contact:

The Coleman Center
810 Seventh Avenue
23rd floor
New York, NY 10019
Tel. 212-541-4600
Fax 212-541-4232
www.ColemanCenter.com
Sales Manager: www.salesmanager@colemancenter.com

Client Comments

"Never have we hosted an event where everything ran so smoothly. The Coleman Center was beyond perfect."

> Meg Mc Bride
> Regulatory Relations Analyst
> The Risk Management Association.

"Thank you for providing us with the best seminar facility in the country. We conduct over 500 company conferences each year. For five years, The Coleman Center has been rated #1 by our attendees."

> Brian McGrath
> Former Chairman
> Executive Enterprises, Inc.

"I recently attended a training session at your fine conference center in New York. I have been involved with international marketing and technical conferences for nearly 15 years in Germany, Italy, England, Japan, Middle East, Holland, France and Switzerland. I have never had the opportunity to be involved with a facility as fine as yours."

> Cyrus Driver
> International Marketing Manager
> Lucent Technology.

"I see why all of our instructors give your staff and the center rave reviews. As you are aware, we have booked sessions for two years ahead. We are so happy to have found the Coleman Center."

> Phyllis J. Olsen
> Manager
> Meetings and Exposition
> World @ Work.

978-0-595-40335-6
0-595-40335-2

www.ingramcontent.com/pod-product-compliance
Lightning Source LLC
Chambersburg PA
CBHW021004180526
45163CB00005B/1889